RESUME BRANDING: 101

Strategies for Getting Noticed in
10 Seconds or Less

SECOND EDITION

KIM N. CARSWELL

ASTA PUBLICATIONS

Published by Asta Publications, LLC
Post Office Box 1735
Stockbridge, Georgia 30281
www.astapublications.com

4/23/14

Printed in the United States of America

Library of Congress Control Number Cataloging-in Publication Data:
2010928062

Carswell, Kim N.
Résumé Branding: 101, Strategies for Getting Noticed in 10 Seconds or Less:

Kim N. Carswell
p.   cm.
ISBN 978-1-934947-49-4
1. Résumé Branding   2. Résumés (Employment) 3.Personal Branding
4. Social Media Marketing   5. Career Transition   6. Outplacement 7. Linkedin 8. Social Media Engagement I. Title

Quotes by Jim Rohn, America's Foremost Business Philosopher, reprinted with permission from Jim Rohn International ©2010.

SECOND EDITION

First Printing 2010

DEDICATION:

This book is dedicated

To my beloved mother Thelma and father Douglas, for your unwavering love, advice and confidence in my abilities – and for setting the standard.

To my hubby Tim, son Kamau and daughters Amaya and Ayanna, for your consistent support and days filled with laughter.

To my extended family of friends, colleagues and the people who know the value of investing in their futures.

CONTENTS

RESUME BRANDING: 101

Strategies for Getting Noticed in 10 Seconds or Less

SECOND EDITION

_____

ACKNOWLEDGMENTS

All thanks be to God who planted another career guidebook within me, and provided the rich experiences over the past three years to add more insight and love into the second edition of Resume Branding 101. He allowed me to be used as a vessel to assist job seekers from various industries and levels of self-esteem. Thank you for letting me "Happy Dance" in their honor.

Kudos to Assuanta F. Howard and her Asta Publications team. Once again you pulled the best out of me... "Well Done." Rachel, Schade you made top-notch edits that surpassed the first book; I appreciate your keen eye.

Special mention to my newest mentor, Denise DeBurst Gines, for your guidance and advice, which always led me back to practicing what I preach when I least expected it.

Gladys, thanks for sitting through hours of workshop commentary and keeping me focused. Jessica I really appreciated your relentless support for sharing this philosophy with your graduate students and monitoring their success.

Ayanna and Amaya, thanks for making sure I received enough rest after long hours of clawing on my laptop. Kamau your comic relief and marketing advice was spot on every time! Tim thanks for supporting me while I traveled the world, retesting the philosophy in new markets for the last three years.

Roy J. Hughley Jr., thanks for calling in the cavalry when I needed it most!

Thanks to the Carswells for the great escape during this year's Thanksgiving weekend. It was the perfect time to put the finishing touches to this book.

Once again, I must take the time to acknowledge all the people who embraced the Resume Branding Strategy™ in their job search and career transition tool box. I tip my hat off to you fir taking control of your brand...

The Best Is Here and Better Is Yet to Come!

Personably,

Kim. N. Carswell

RESUME BRANDING: 101

Strategies for Getting Noticed in 10 Seconds or Less

SECOND EDITION

1

THE CPR OF BRANDING

"Character is like a tree and reputation like a shadow. The shadow is what we think of it; the tree is the real thing." – Abraham Lincoln

Understanding the power of a brand and how it will breathe life into your job search is invaluable. When I first began to use the branding term 7 years ago, people would greet me with a deer-caught-in-headlights look. "Huh?" They just did not get it.

Fast forward to the present and you cannot swim through all of the daily branding references without a timeout to catch your breath. For the sake of readers who are still not there yet...

Corporate Model

Marty Neumeier, author of The Brand Gap, defines brand as "a person's gut feeling about a product, service or organization. It's not what you think it is...it's what they say it is." This is the essence of Business Branding. It is a vital function which differentiates one business from another. Branding a business involves a laundry list of all the features and experiences one may encounter when interacting with the company, such as the look, feel, and customer care. The combination of the shape, size and color of a company's logo, its website, its mission statement, and products and services all help a potential customer decide the company's value.

Personal Model

Personal branding involves the essence of who you are and how to market your personality, credentials, and experience to the world. It's your reputation and what people say about you when you leave the room. It's what people say about you when they have to describe you to peers, colleagues or people in their professional networks.

At first glance, many people frowned upon this notion because it felt inhumane, distant, and trivial. Once career experts began embracing the concept of marketing one's skills set, advising job seekers to evaluate who they are and what they want, and exploring ways to reach one's employment goals, people started to warm up to the idea.

People who know their personal brands are getting hired more often and faster, despite the state of the economy; 7% is still high in my book (pun intended). The overarching goal of personal branding is to bank on the fact that we create our own economy.

Resume Model

For over 29 years, I have been helping people gain advanced employment by writing customized resumes and training them on ways to promote themselves in the workplace. When I founded Persona Affairs, I made the decision to streamline the way people branded their personas and their businesses. Therefore, it was a natural progression for us to take resume writing a step further by merging the nuances of each branding type and designing a Resume Branding Strategy™ that incorporates marketing techniques into a viable job search approach.

We coined the Resume Branding term to redefine how to add value to today's resume writing process. Far too many tips, blogs, and articles share ways to "fill in" a document or write what I like to call "mini job descriptions."

We have a saying at Persona: "While everyone is trying to get on the same page, we are on the 'Same Paragraph.™' This is because if I am at the bottom of the page and you are at the top, then things can get lost in translation. Basically, there is a disconnection. " In branding, one's message has to be accurate, clear, and consistent.

When branding a resume, it is essential to capture your persona on paper. Most likely you're walking around with a resume that does not tell your story or worth because you have an outdated template and old advice. We used the Same Paragraph™ motto to create an innovative approach to introduce and rewire our "employer-friendly" resume format. When branding a person, there is no room for errors or misinterpretations. Reputations ride on a concise and compelling reflection of your talents and abilities.

As the quote by Abraham Lincoln at the beginning of the chapter indicates, your character is the source of your reputation. With personal branding you have the opportunity to steer the course of how others judge your character after meeting you for the first time--whether it happens to be in person, on paper, or online.

Hence, branding is an emotional connection to a sustainable business in the future. For the purposes of defining the Resume Branding Strategy,™ the goal is to create employment invitations by generating positive responses from potential employers within ten seconds and getting paid more in the end.

What in your past experiences can be useful in today's market? Does your resume reflect a solid pattern of accomplishments, or does it hide employment gaps? Resume Branding is not a "smoke and mirrors" trick; it is more substantive than that.

To get a clearer picture, let's introduce Resume Branding by what it is not. It is not an elevator pitch, personal brand statement, picture, or online profile. More strategy is involved in developing a cohesive brand identity; one has to take into consideration one's competition, employer demographics, corporate culture, and what talents he or she can offer to an employer that other candidates cannot.

Resume Branding is a totality of visual identity, credentials, operations, and social interactions; it is the essence of combining business and emotional characteristics to relay a core concept, message, or transaction. Therefore, when branding yourself, consider which transferable skill sets you want potential employers to walk away with.

There is a spiritual saying: "Are you your brother's keeper?" Well, in the personal branding world, "Are you the customer's keeper?"

The first saying makes us responsible for our fellow (wo) man, whereas the latter shifts your onus to keeping your employer's brand promise to its clients.

Employers are in business because they have a customer base to build and maintain. How do you retain clients by your brand promise? Are you the "go-to" person when a problem arises? Do co-workers pick you as the leader for big projects or as the group's spokesperson? Who are you and why are you important to your employer or profession? Your resume should answer these questions.

A Japanese system called "Kaizen" is used by many companies to preserve their brand promises and maintain effective levels of customer satisfaction from all echelons within a business. Kaizen practitioners solicit input from employees in diverse areas of a company to obtain well-rounded feedback about how well internal operations are achieving business goals. In Resume Branding, the purpose is to elevate your accomplishments and core competencies so that employers are willing to explore whether or not you will fit into their corporate family, and how well you can contribute to the success of the company and keep driving customers through the door.

In the business world, people are captivated with ideal truths and concerned about what others think. Resume Branding is an "out–of-body" experience, because when you create a resume, you are packaging it from an outsider's perspective, while maintaining the essence of who you are.

This is why brand strategists and marketing departments are feverishly crafting ways to gain our attention. They're hired to interpret and predict what sells.

On the other hand, with Resume Branding Strategy™ the reverse notion is true. The primary focus is directed toward who we are professionally, how we can consistently prove it, and lastly, how people (potential employers) may share in our valued experiences. When building an employable brand, the end, or resume, must justify the means, or job offer. Are you ready to read on and learn ways to quickly earn more? I certainly hope so.

When branding a resume, it is crucial for the writer and reader to speak the same language. For the purposes of this guidebook, Resume Branding is a true assessment tool for successfully showcasing a professional's value by blending previous work experiences with individual personality. But first you must revisit past accomplishments to gain insight on ways to market your expertise on paper, and then establish a digital voice and footprint through social media. The ultimate goal is to get hired faster and earn more from the start. 97% of our resume branding clients are employed and make an average of $10,000 more than their colleagues.

How to Prove your Value

According to world-renowned motivational speaker (one of my favorites) Jim Rohn, "You don't get paid for the hour; you get paid for the value you bring to the hour." This profound statement forces you to not only look at yourself in the mirror differently, but to also press the pause button. Stop spinning your "I-have-to-find-another-job" wheels and start looking at your past employment choices for clues to find your ideal job situation.

You might have an idea of what you would like to be paid per hour or annually, but what justifies your worth? Can you pinpoint why you should be the top candidate for every position you apply to? Or do you think being qualified is good enough before hitting the "Submit" button?

In far too many cases, job seekers do not determine a market value for their past work history. Employers will not help you,- nor should they. Some applicants are fortunate enough to be asked for their salary requirements during the application stage. But most sell themselves short even when this occurs.

Take a look in the mirror. What do you see? Ask yourself about the thoughts that cross your mind. Are you settling? Can you negotiate for more money? Do you hear a private internal voice or others' voices saying you are not good enough?

It may appear odd to ask a value-based question in a Resume Branding book, but if you carry others' interpretations of yourself, then you treasure their opinions, despite whether they are true or positive. So what is your value and how did you determine it?

Resume Branding Strategy™ consolidates both traditional professional career writing techniques and modern personal branding strategies to reduce the job search period and attract a higher starting salary than the competition.

How and why information is placed on a resume is a prudent question to answer for employers. Who is the intended audience? Why would they find your experience useful? How much time does it take to read 200-1000 resumes? With Resume Branding, these questions are answered to create an "employer-friendly" brand that is mirrored in the final product.

Consequently, branding is more than a product. In brand development there is a common scenario that occurs when we define what constitutes a brand. If we look at the Coca-Cola Company®, we find that its brand is worth 68.73 billion dollars. If Coca-Cola shut down its global production plants today and laid off all of its employees (hopefully this will never happen), the company would still be worth billions of dollars. Why? Because according to Allen Adamson of Landor Associates, a branding firm, "A well-honed brand evokes in consumers an emotion, and a promise of what it will deliver, without the customer having to do much." That's brand value; we envision the experience, know what we are promised, and maintain a memorable impression about the company's product or service.

Resume Branding is a unique process that fuses your business value, brand promise, and personality into a marketable document. It also serves as the foundation for building a strong online presence and platform to define your digital voice.

Ask yourself what you want others to know about you from a professional standpoint. Why should a business trust you with its secret recipe for success? What are you prepared to bring to the table besides a knife, fork and an empty stomach? Why should an employer create a flourishing environment for you to prosper in? Your personal brand should answer all of these questions within a short period of time. If it does not, then you are engaging in a futile exercise of devaluing yourself and risking being misplaced for the sake of paying a few bills.

CHAPTER 1 COMMENTARY REFLECTIONS

1. In five words, describe your personal brand.

2. What five words would your co-workers use to describe you?

2

RESUME BRANDING IS MORE THAN A NAME

"Philosophy is like trying to open a safe with a combination lock: each little adjustment of the dials seems to achieve nothing, only when everything is in place does the door open." ~ *Ludwig Wittgenstein*

A lot has happened since my first edition of Resume Branding 101 appeared in the US job market. For the past three years, my personal branding firm, Persona Affairs, has prepared thousands of job seekers and professionals for the well-anticipated change in how employers are hiring top talent. Along with stepping up our social media engagement efforts, we polled human resource managers on what traits they're looking for in an ideal candidate.

During this time we have hosted and facilitated hundreds of resume branding workshops, social media seminars, interview mapping, and resume reviewing sessions to help people elevate their understanding of how to best demonstrate their value and brand presence on and offline. The key term is "brand."

I have watched countless professionals stumble throughout the job search process without knowing their true market value or where to sell it. They're like hamsters trying to get off their wheels without knowing how to put on the brakes. It is time to STOP running in circles and continue reading the rest of this book.

Juggling financial burdens and fighting the urge to apply for every position that crosses your path is a dreadful reality for many. Frustration is preventing highly qualified candidates from throwing a hat into the employment ring and, ultimately, their hands up in triumph.

Understanding why job seekers do what they do is important, but I prefer to spend most of my energy educating readers with the answers to the "why not" questions. Don't you think it is time to latch onto proven methods that will make your personality stand out from the crowd of desperate and not- so- desperate job seekers? If you are reading this book, the answer most likely is yes. Good news...

The Second Edition of Resume Branding 101 is here, the tide has now turned, and employers are hiring again. Let's look at the numbers. In 2009, the unemployment rate was 10%, and as of May 2013 it's at 7%. This is an excellent time for the unemployed, underemployed, and working professionals who are ready to take their careers to the next level. The key term is "ready."

As you are getting prepared, please keep in mind that if you're in a minority group, the national unemployment rate for you is double what it is for those in non-minority groups. Therefore, it is important to keep reading to glean a better understanding of how to improve your chances. Adopting a new thought process on how to write a marketable resume will help you walk away with a proven social media engagement strategy in this post-recession job market and make more money than the competition.

With that said, my main goal in writing this book is to share the truth about the hiring process from the employer's perspective. Employers are in the business of weeding out weak and generic applicants. The first stage is to scan through the resumes and toss whoever's is least fit for the position. In most cases, it is the ones whose resumes look the worst. They are ones that lack personality and are filled with paragraphs that scream, "Blah, blah blah... I'll take anything."

This book is NOT about creating pretty resumes or sprinkling a handful of buzzwords (although a branded resume has both elements) all over the place. Put it down if you want another template to copy and slap your name on top.... That's cheating yourself and your overall earning potential.

The Second Edition of Resume Branding 101 speaks to readers in plain terms about executing proven personal branding strategies for getting noticed in the post-recession job market. Not from a gimmicky perspective, but from a position of trust, honesty, and results. I want to help job seekers consider all of their options and not settle for positions that are not aligned with their career personalities. I wrote this book to make you the top candidate for the roles that best match your talents, abilities, and past performance so that employers will pay you at least 10% more than your competitors.

As a certified mediator, employer, and former recruiter (yes, I've worn many hats), it is easy for me to understand both sides of the hiring table. I know the desires of an anxious candidate and I empathize with employers' needs. After sitting with countless job seekers in the interview process, I can tell the difference between the ones that know their stuff versus those who are seasoned interviewees that think canned responses will speak to the job at hand. These days employers are tech savvy and use behavioral-based questions to elicit your core values and articulated skill set.

The Resume Branding process meets everyone in the middle, but only works for people who are ready to see themselves in a marketable light. Hopefully, you will realize that these proven Resume Branding Strategy™ and social media tools can land you the job of your dreams. Stop spinning on that hamster wheel. It's time for something new.

CHAPTER 2 COMMENTARY REFLECTIONS

1. In what ways do you provide value?

2. What makes you indispensable?

3. What do you consider to be your professional strengths? Give me specific examples using these attributes in the work-place

PART 1

DISCOVERY

3

RESUME BRANDING PHILOSOPHY

"Our character is basically a composite of our habits. Because they are consistent, often unconscious patterns, they constantly, daily, express our character.. " - Stephen Covey

Job seekers often leave their storytelling for the face-to-face interview, in hopes of getting the opportunity to spell out how they are best suited for the vacant position. Unfortunately, with today's competitive environment, waiting until later is not an option. The Resume Branding Strategy™ includes five core principles to help you create a marketable "employer-friendly" resume and career-related documents that make it easier to compete and earn more money than your competitors:

1. The Resume Is a First Interview
2. The Resume Is an Invitation
3. The Resume Tells Your Brand Story
4. The Resume Is for the Reader and Not the Writer
5. The Resume Can be Scanned in ten Seconds or Less

Part of a seasoned resume writer's responsibility is to pose questions such as, "Why would someone want to interview you? What makes you unique to hiring managers?" The answers cannot be based on desperation, financial obligations (i.e. bills to pay), the need to get out of a "toxic" environment, or the fact that you are on an internal quest toward finding "what I want to do in life." The resume must reflect who you are and why you are applying for each job.

Unfortunately, most resume writers have never been on the other side of the employment process, so they fail to ask the most pressing questions that address employers' needs. However, they know how to plug your personal information into a template, talk to you for an hour, and 24 hours later, produce a new resume. This is not enough. You need a marketable document that has the employer and hiring staff in mind.

People and systems that scan job applications need to see a clear and concise reflection of your market value on a resume. They should not ask, "Why did this person apply to this position?" or think, "This person must be desperate, because his/her resume is too generic." It may seem evident that I am taking a hiring manager's perspective, but this position is an important deviation from the normal route of a resume writer. Shifting the focus from applicant-centered to employer-friendly is a pivotal change that provides a strategy to garner a higher return on your investment.

Job seekers are constantly putting themselves in a vulnerable position. Of course, they have the power to control which jobs and/or positions to apply to, but once that decision is made, the onus falls on the electronic scanner or person reading the resume to determine a job candidate's market value. Why not give hiring managers what they desire versus listing items or buzzwords that only make you feel satisfied? It is not enough to qualify for a job; you have to demonstrate that you're better than any other applicant and that your salary should be higher than that of the rest.

Another aspect to consider is that a resume should make you feel accomplished. Likewise, it must be easily discernible to people who know nothing about you or the companies you've worked for. Even if your current or former employer is a well-branded Fortune 500 company, you ought to consider whether or not everyone is familiar with certain divisions or niche departments within that company. In most instances, the answer will be "No." Readers of your resume need to quickly solicit your goals and have a clear understanding of what transferable skill sets are being brought to the table-- in ten seconds or less.

CHAPTER 3 COMMENTARY REFLECTIONS

1.   Do your qualifications invite the reader to place your resume in the "Phone/In-Person Interview" stack within ten seconds?

2.   Is the length appropriate for professional or executive level positions?

3.   Does your resume reveal a brand story?

4

RESUME BRAND PURPOSE

First Interview

"Interview, Don't clamor for an interview. Instead search for the INNER VIEW. " ~ Sri Sathya Sai Baba

Resume Branding: How is it different from standard resume writing techniques? The Resume Branding Strategy™ is based on a firm foundation in traditional methods of writing and advertising, along with a strategic approach to compete, engage, and earn more money in today's competitive job market. Both unemployed and underemployed job seekers are bombarded with conflicting messages about how to best structure a resume. As a result of the recent economic crisis, millions of people around the country find themselves looking for stable companies to transition into.

With hopes and promises of new careers in "green technology jobs" designed for supplementing the declining auto industry and emaciated real estate market, learning to master your brand persona on paper is a timely subject.

In addition to hearing new buzzwords crafted every day by marketers, people want and need practical guidance about how to make beneficial career choices. Recently displaced workers are finding themselves examining what brings them temporary stability versus pursuing their passion or purpose. The notion of highlighting the "brandividual" is an essential marketing tool for people to separate themselves from the pack of competitors. According to David Armano, who originally coined the term, a "'brandividual' is an individual employee who draws on her or his personal identity, as well as the organization or brand's identity, to represent the organization or brand in online relationships." Resume Branding allows you to broadcast your past, passion, and purpose on paper.

Branding experts have also suggested that job seekers include personal branding techniques when writing their resumes and creating online profiles on social networks such as Facebook, Twitter, and LinkedIn. However, it was not until 2003 that the art of resume composition and branding techniques were integrated. After years of writing resumes and creating competitive documents, I decided to incorporate specific personal branding strategies into a career transition tool. The Resume Branding Strategy™ is the blending of two ideologies into one easily adaptable philosophy for your resume to be competitive and attractive to everyone who sees it.

If this sounds challenging, you're in luck, because you have taken the first step by reading Resume Branding 101. This guidebook will explain not only the "why," but also the "who," "what," "when," "how," and, most of all, the "why not" for maximizing your personality, talents, and experiences into a marketable resume. Most resume writing books include a litany of templates showing you how to fill in a resume, but fail to fully explain the "what, why, and how" to make your resume competitive for today's job market. Resume Branding answers those questions because I have been on both sides of the hiring table. After spending nearly three decades tweaking and perfecting resumes, I have found how one can combine and add personality, competitiveness, and past accomplishments into a cohesive resume format, tailored for a robust job search process.

It was during my tenure as a Graduate Admissions Committee member at one of the top five MBA schools in the United States, that I instated the final component of the Resume Branding Matrix Format,™ as outlined in Chapter 11 of this book. After becoming a recruiter, I experienced a huge paradigm shift. I began making resumes with the reader's time and expectations in mind, rather than just writing a well-articulated document to fulfill an application's requirements.

In addition, I spelled out the quantitative and qualitative portions of outlining a corporate resume. When I successfully evaluated thousands of international credentials and curricula vitae from 75 countries into one readable format for the Master's Admissions Committee, I knew I had found the missing link that could be applied to every resume structure.

A crucial component of Resume Branding was to develop a cosmic companion or universal draw to today's job market needs. It is reflective of a much-needed paradigm shift from submitter-centered to hiring manager-focused resumes. It may seem like this philosophy contradicts the personal branding aspect of resume writing, but diverting attention toward the reader serves a greater purpose.

In retrospect, one may ask the question, "Why take the time to put one's talents and diverse skill sets into a resume if it's only focused on the recruiter or talent manager?" Well, remember the five Resume Branding mantras which were implemented for the distinct purpose of creating dynamic and reactive resumes. The top two are "The Resume Is the First Interview" and "The Resume Is an Invitation."

There are many people who want to skip this first step by saving the "good stuff" for the interview and transforming their resumes into "mini-job descriptions." I often share with our clients that if you do not get past the initial visual and/or electronic scanning process, then you will not get an in-person or phone interview, and ultimately, will not get hired. Once you have decided where to submit your resume, do not wait for the second phase of the job application process to bring out your personality; it will be too late. Recruiters and talent acquisition managers often say that "if you cannot be found on Google then you do not exist." With that in mind, we merged the need for an engaging brand story with an attractive digital footprint.

Remember, the power of leaving a positive first impression is critical. Personalities must have a dominant presence in resumes. Job seekers should shift their focus from following protocol to drafting marketable documents with potential employers in mind. Consequently, the writing portion is far more difficult if you do not know what message to send. This message should answer the question, "What is your Brand Story?" It's time to discover your business persona and market value.

CHAPTER 4 COMMENTARY REFLECTIONS

1.   What are your feelings toward the idea that "if you are not online, you do not exist?"

2.   What is your brand promise?

3.   Does your brand promise relate to the positions and industries in which you are seeking employment? If the answer is "no," why not?

4. Does your current resume answer why are you the best candidate for the position listed in the job description?

5. Does your brand promise relate to the positions and industries in which you are seeking employment? If the answer is "no", why not?

5

BRAND YOU CAN TRUST

An Invitation

"The way to gain a good reputation is to endeavor to be what you desire to appear." ~ Socrates

Not only is it best to consider your document as the first interview, but also you should use it to prepare for all stages of the interview process. Get past the first stage and make your resume inviting. Yes, treat your resume like an invitation. Take a look at your current resume and examine your introduction versus the Microsoft Word template you used. Does yours appear to be the same as billions of others' who have filled out a Microsoft Word template? Perhaps yes, because templates are confining and make it extremely difficult to bring out your personality.

How many times did you attempt to fit your text into a template that would not allow it? As a person with diverse experiences and accomplishments, a confined outline will limit your ability to stand out from the crowd. The ultimate goal is to get noticed, not to allow the recipient to readily identify which template you used.

In addition, realize that the notion of making your resume into an invitation does not imply that one should cram it onto one page. On average, "single-page" resumes are for persons with less than five to seven years of experience. There will always be exceptions to this rule, just based on the basic premise that we are all unique and possess a different set of work histories and credentials, but in general, when professionals scale down their resumes to fit onto one page, they are ultimately cutting themselves off at the knees. The main reason behind the one-pager is to make the document concise and to provide a limit to a litany of pages.

Understanding your brand value and investigating the benefits of meeting your potential employer's needs is essential. In addition to seeing one's value on the appropriate number of pages, job seekers must start to envision themselves driving to the location and walking through the parking lot, or, for those who are trying to transition within the same company, pressing the elevator button to the new floor every day. Can you adjust to the new department's setup and culture? All of these mental exercises allow the job seeker to feel a sense of empowerment as she or he goes through the job search or career transition, to learn the nuances of where she or he wants to work, and to explore how to make her or his brand persona stand out within that vision. The ultimate goal is to pass the screening process, find an advocate in the hiring process, and be in the position to walk into a future employment situation.

Bringing the message back to your resume, the document must mirror the tone of these exercises. Once again, "The Resume Is the First Interview." Many organizations have a team or panel of people who come together to determine which of the applicants would be a good fit for the company. This means that your resume has to resonate with everyone who touches the document and invite them to align their personal brand with yours. If you do not make it through the screening phase, you will not reach the next series of contact interviews. However, this is not an invitation to spill your guts on a "two-page" resume with size eight font, or worse yet, on a one-pager. Treat the entire document as a sales sheet, which begins with a sales (or elevator) pitch for top candidacy, and ends with a complete snapshot of your transferable skill sets.

CHAPTER 5 COMMENTARY REFLECTIONS

1.   Can you describe your strongest skill sets?

2. Which industry and/or positions is your resume designed to attract?

3.   Examine your resume and list the missing components that make it less competitive.

4. What do you envision your next job to be?

6

PEACE OF MIND

A Brand Story

"Looking back you realize that a very special person passed briefly through your life and it was you. It is not too late to find that person again." - Robert Brault

In most instances, when people attempt to get a new position, they are putting their best foot forward. Unfortunately in today's tough market, you need to put on a pair of socks and sneakers, because your new employer needs someone to hit the ground running from day one. It is no longer time for job seekers to test the market. The market in itself is a test; a test of will, determination, and most importantly, strategy.

Outlining your credentials is one of the initial steps required to assemble a positive 10-second impression. What are you coming to the hiring table with, besides a knife and fork? What are you prepared to make to accompany the company "meal?" The market is full of qualified chefs, but it is the task of job candidates to find the company which best fits their ideal cuisine choice. How will you whet the appetite of a potential employer and encourage them to invite you to the table?

As you can tell, I love food analogies, but these examples should ring true. It is important to see the Resume Branding Strategy™ as a simple tool to achieve employment success. People must take the time to outline their credentials. Evaluating qualifications is not limited to education. The goal is to find the core of what's been done in your past and present it in the most marketable light.

Look back and think about the first person to shape your thoughts about the world of work. What appealed to you about your first, second, or third job? Why did you choose to study certain topics in school? Where were you most successful? How do you plan to compete in today's job market? This exercise should ultimately reveal a plausible direction for your professional future. Consciously appraise your formal education, employment history, On-the-Job Training (OJT), and accomplishments to expose your brand story.

In the Resume Brand Matrix Format™ section in Chapter 11 of this guidebook, you will be taught how to clearly identify professional deeds you performed above and beyond what you were hired to do, i.e., accomplishments/ impact. According to the pioneer brand story developer Mark Thomson, "Brands are the stories that unite us all in a common purpose within an enterprise, and connect us with the people we serve on the outside." A brand story depicts the essence of what a person is known for.

For a job seeker to obtain a contact interview, he or she must create a well-branded resume which features his or her beginning, middle, and overall potential. What in your past makes you a good fit for this position? Why are you interested in leaving your current job or industry? What about this company makes you fit to join the team? And if you are unemployed, what in your employment experience is strong enough to overshadow your current status? These questions should be answered in your brand story. Where is the best place to read this story? In your resume.

Here is My Brand Story:

The people who framed my thoughts about the world of work were my parents, Douglas and Thelma Howard. My father was an executive for Macy's department store, the iconic American retailing brand located on 34th Street in Manhattan, New York. It is not a coincidence that "Miracle on 34th Street" is my all-time favorite Christmas movie. Apart from learning the importance of quality, following through on tasks, and the intricate role fashion played in presenting a polished appearance in the workplace, he taught me the basics of dictating the direction of my personal brand.

On the other hand, my mother had a more practical set of lessons for me to gravitate towards. She was a stay-at-home mom who returned to work and started her collegiate career while I was in junior high school. Her thirst for knowledge afforded me the opportunity to witness how one juggles family, career transition, and educational pursuits from a non-traditional student's perspective. Once I reached high school, my mother worked as an adjunct professor who taught an ad-hoc lesson regarding the "Fundamentals of Resume Writing."

Prior to turning fifteen, I knew that I wanted to work for the infamous "quick serve" giant: McDonald's in Darien, Connecticut. The pay was superb and they provided bus transportation to their new restaurant located on Interstate 95. I was hired a few days after my fifteenth birthday, excelled in customer service, and built camaraderie between coworkers that has lasted for decades. Thanks to Facebook, we are still in contact today.

My second employment experience was during my senior year in high school as an Executive Intern with a real estate attorney who practiced on Park Avenue in New York City. There I witnessed multimillion dollar transactions and learned the importance of positive conflict management approaches when things do not go as planned.

Finally, my third job was working a dual role in the Investigation and Actuarial Science departments at the New York State Insurance Fund. Consequently, helping mom critique resumes truly paid off. I knew how to identify my transferable skill sets by the mere age of sixteen, and have been writing resumes ever since!

After transferring my administrative abilities to various industries such as transportation, printing, and corrections, I decided to relocate to Atlanta, Georgia, to attend college. Thanks to Mom's blueprint and Daddy's work ethic (yes, I'm still a daddy's girl), I attended Georgia State University (GSU) as a non-traditional student, single parent, and part-time student assistant. Fortunately, within a three-month period, a supervisory position presented itself and I began working in the Financial Aid office, inherited a staff of twenty-two individuals, and continued to help fellow coworkers and classmates re-write their resumes along the way.

Originally, my thoughts were to major in business management when I started at GSU, given that I had eight years of work experience under my belt. However, when I took a closer examination of the program of study, I saw that I would have to take courses such as Decision Sciences, Accounting, and Finance. Since mathematics was never my strong suit, I focused my talents and passions toward speaking, learning how people transition in the world, and resolving both workplace and international conflicts. Ultimately, I graduated with a Bachelor of Arts degree in Communications with a minor in Sociology, pursued a Master's Degree in Conflict Management from Kennesaw State University, and earned certifications in Kingian Nonviolence Conflict Reconciliation from The University of Rhode Island and Emory University in Atlanta.

One of my early career branding experiences was working with domestic and international students in Graduate Admissions and Undergraduate Recruitment. In this supervisory capacity, I executed both corporate and personal branding strategies within an educational environment. It is important to understand that on one hand, I was able to critique resumes and credentials from around the world, and on the other hand, I was able to use my branding experience to help new international students in their transition into the American university system. Simultaneously, I was also educating and providing domestic students with actionable strategies to secure financial aid and scholarship assistance.

As I look back, my foundation was built on a diverse pattern of experiences that helped determine my life's purpose. Every position, conflict, and course attributed to why I started my own business and decided three years ago to write Resume Branding 101, a career guidebook to communicate and teach people how to brand themselves in today's competitive market.

The ultimate challenge in resume writing is to take a snapshot of your brand story and scale it down to be told in under ten seconds. In Chapter 11, you will see a sample of how my brand story is revised within the "Summary of Qualifications" section. Again, the goal is to be noticed by all who touch or have access to your document. You want everyone to have a succinct and consistent idea of your talents and transferable skill sets. Far too often, people say, "I do not know how to put it on paper, but if you get me into the interview, I can tell you more." Or, "I do not know how to put it into words, but if they give me a chance, I can show them." What recruiter really has time for that when she or he is sorting through thousands of resumes? What if you're incorrect or have not done extensive research to learn the intricacies of the job? As a general rule, the objective is to put it on paper. Remember, "The Resume Is the First Interview."

Adding personality to a resume makes it much easier to showcase your credentials and to stand out in a competitive market. It is important to accept your limitations. If you find that writing a resume is too difficult, then reinvest in your brand and pay a professional resume writer to renovate your resume. However, we suggest using the Resume Branding

Matrix Format™ outlined in Chapter 11. Yes, I said pay someone to compose a professional resume. Think about the salary you wish to make, take 1% of that, and invest it into building a better personality on paper. Are you worth a fraction of your potential salary?

CHAPTER 6 COMMENTARY REFLECTIONS

1.   What is your brand story?

2.   Do you see a pattern in your past that can be applied to your future employment goals?

3.   How would you rate your educational background? Is there room for improvement?

7

A BRAND NEW SALE

Reader Not The Writer

"If we all did the things we are capable of doing, we would literally astound ourselves.." ~ Thomas A. Edison

Some may say, "I do not know how to sell myself!" or, "I am not a salesperson." Well, how does one get the message across about their skill sets and talents without selling their soul?

A marketeer's approach to selling includes understanding the product's strengths and benefits and promoting them to the community that needs the product.

A similar tactic can be used by job-seeking populations. Being aware of your abilities, goals, strengths, and preferred corporate climate will highlight avenues of employment. What is the best environment for you to be successful in? "Seek and you shall find." However, when you find the best fit, how will you relay your desire and level of expertise in ten seconds or less? This is the main premise of the Resume Branding Strategy;™ how one can demonstrate that she or he fits the criteria and let her or his personality direct the next course of action.

Getting noticed and hired fast are the job seeker's goals. As the initial strategy in Resume Branding suggests, "The Resume Is the First Interview." Consequently, if you do not make it beyond the sorting and/or scanning process, you will not get the second interview or the job. Furthermore, the "fill-in" and "mini-job description" approaches do not work.

Resume Branding 101 outlines a successful strategy to get your document past the administrative assistant to the decision maker's attention. They will notice your credentials and ultimately your personal brand value within seconds. You may ask, "How is this done in such a short period of time?" Well, it is all in the format. Later in the book we will break down the finer elements of designing a branded resume. It's not only for your benefit, but also for the benefit of the reader.

How will you demonstrate effectively that you are the best fit for the job posted? Does your resume reveal your desperation? From a hiring manager's perspective, the desperation question is easily answered by the following: Did you find a few items listed on the job description that you have direct experience with, while overlooking other aspects of the position? Did you pluck a few key words from the job description and sprinkle them into your resume? The reader will get whatever energy you put into the document. If I had a dollar for every resume I've seen with text cut and pasted from a job description or a sample resume, I would be a millionaire. Analyze the position you wish to apply to, and if eighty-to-ninety percent of what they are looking for matches your skill sets and work history, then by all means, go for it. But if it does not, you are asking for a rejected application and a longer job search period.

In addition to not knowing the industry you are applying to, the resume type used can diminish your ability to become noticed. Did you get a resume template from Microsoft Word, Monster, or CareerBuilder? There is nothing wrong with using templates; however, they do not address the personal branding needs of today's competitive job market. They follow protocol, but do not add personality. Templates address the basic needs of a resume (aesthetics), but not the needs of employers.

The Resume Branding Matrix Format™ was designed to assist professionals who need help showcasing their talents and desires without listing the antiquated "Objective Statement." How and when to include an objective statement is a long-standing dilemma among resume writers and career advisors. My company stopped writing them over eighteen years ago because they state what job seekers want from the employer before they have demonstrated their brand value.

Another major mistake is to assume that the first person to review the resume is a decision maker. Far too often it is not. It may be the company's gatekeeper, such as an administrative assistant or desk clerk within the Human Resources Department. Therefore, the format used to express your expertise, transferable skill sets, and personality must be appealing to the gatekeeper.

Although they may not know the intricacies of each vacant position, the resume must easily highlight that you have the appropriate experience. The goal is to alert the reader in ten seconds or less that you are worthy enough to align their personal/internal brand with your candidacy. Ideally you want everyone in the hiring process to become an advocate because your resume demonstrates that you're a good fit for the organization.

Therefore, the resume must translate beyond the submission stage and into the candidate stage. Do not assume that riddling the resume with random key words will gain speedy access; it may get your document into the infamous "File #13."

There is a saying stating that "you should not worry about things you cannot control." To add a spiritual perspective, "You cannot pray and worry at the same time." I often tell my clients that they must be honest on their resumes. Far too often, people add erroneous information or omit details from their resumes in hopes of customizing their documents for each position. For example, in one of my career coaching LinkedIn groups, a resume writer suggested typing keywords at the bottom of a page and changing the font color to white so that it can remain hidden if printed. Her goal was to trick an electronic scanner into producing a favorable reading, to pass the resume on to the next level. Unfortunately, this is not the best way to tailor a resume for prolonged success.

Tell the truth gracefully and focus on your strengths, not your weaknesses. If job seekers have a checkered past and/ or gaps, appropriate honesty is the best approach to use. The goal of the Resume Branding Format™ is to highlight individual talents and marketable transferable skill sets versus directing attention to challenging work patterns.

Furthermore, the employment content must be balanced to satisfy the needs of each scanning audience. . The second page is often read once you make it out of the initial scanning phase. Keep the reader in mind when designing your resume. Can a person access your brand persona while taking phone calls or sifting through 500 resumes?

Resume Branding is the solution. Oftentimes, people tend to focus only on the writing portion. However, the writing is one of the last pieces of the puzzle. First, one must determine the target audience.

Which company and employment cultures will fit your personality and professional outlook? Second, people often fail to research; they want the first thing that comes down the pipe. If you are taking the time to send out twenty resumes, hopefully they are twenty customized resumes that are targeted to each position. Employers are egotistical. They want to feel that they're your first employment choice. It appears that job seekers are asking, "Why should I exhaust myself with customizing a resume each time?" In an effort to save time and energy most job seekers kill their chances of getting hired when they fail to brand themselves from the start. By skipping the research step and jumping into the job market, you are employing "Spaghetti on the Wall" strategy, which means you are throwing everything at a wall to see what sticks. This approach increases your rejection rate, and adds more time and heartache to an already gut-wrenching process.

Don't be a time-waster. It is a huge nuisance for someone to sift through desperate attempts from job seekers who want companies to pay them based on the fact that they are in need of a job. Employers are not concerned about your unemployment. Their first priority is to fill vacant positions with the most qualified candidates.

CHAPTER 7 COMMENTARY REFLECTIONS

1.   How do you plan to make your resume concise without leaving out critical information?

2.   Can you find information on your resume that can be saved for an-in contact interview? List those items here:

3.   What are the most common key phrases or buzzwords in your industry?

8

A BRAND PERSONA

10 Seconds or Less

"Try not to become a person of success, but try to become a person of value."
~ Albert Einstein

What are you known for? Do you complete your work in an unnervingly speedy manner or an extremely efficient way? Remember when you were in school and there was always that person who finished tests first? Or maybe you were that person. Thirty years later at a class reunion, former classmates rekindle stories about that guy who almost broke his neck trying to prevent others from turning in their tests before him. Well those character behaviors are part of a personal brand; consistent attributes which can be ascribed to a series of personality traits are the building blocks to all brands.

A commonly used concept in business is the power of perception. I never liked this word because it is often misused by persons with ill-intent. They often sway perception to their advantage by sending out false readings of a rival's brand.

Think about a colleague who has a poor work ethic yet has the boss's ear. How often does this person divert attention from his or her lack of productivity and direct it to you? Though it may sound out of place for the purposes of this book, it is important to have the power of perception when beginning the personal branding process; it will be easier to define and protect your brand value well beyond the hiring stage. In Dr. Phil McGraw's new bestselling book called Life Code: The New Rules for Winning in the Real World, he writes about how toxic people often move up in a company because they pay more attention to their bosses by using tactics to exploit you and take what is yours professionally. It's time to take control of your brand and set the tone for the rest of your career.

The Resume Branding Strategy™ outlines how to develop a well-defined personal brand that will conquer any harmful tactics and steer you in the direction of your employment choice. Most importantly, you will have a better appreciation for your talents. Once you have researched your industry, you will cultivate the credentials that will assist you in climbing a targeted career ladder.

What are your skill sets? From a professional standpoint, what are you good at? Returning back to one of my favorite brands, here is another Coca-Cola analogy. In 2008, it was declared as the number one brand in the world by Interbrand; therefore, Coke has unique traits that keep it on top. For example, if you were in a restaurant and ordered a Coke but it had a flat taste, would you blame Coca-Cola for the flavor? Or would you blame the establishment? Your first thought would probably be to alert the server that there is something wrong with "their" Coke. In most cases, variations of the product reside with the retailer and not the cola giant, which is known for a consistent look, feel, taste, and level of quality. That's a brand persona you can trust.

The challenge with evaluating an individual's brand persona is that one has to start by asking questions from a sample of people around that individual. One of my favorite interview questions is: "If I were to ask a colleague about you, what would she or he say?" The purpose of this inquiry goes back to the power of perception, your market value, and brand promise.

When I met the Chief Diversity Officer of Coca-Cola, Steve Bucherati at the 2010 Diversity Roundtable, we discussed my approach to Resume Branding and the time it takes to notice great talent. He shared with me his screening process and thoughts on how much time job seekers really have to make a first impression. He shared, "You only have ten seconds, really. If the resume is good, then you get another twenty."

His sentiments directly correlated with my resume formatting philosophy and added fuel to writing the Resume Branding 101 guidebook. With Resume Branding, a person must take a value assessment of his or her stock. Let's take a closer look at what ingredients make up a successful professional. Conduct a personal inventory control exercise on your level of experience, abilities, and talents for the position you seek. What similar traits are present?

CHAPTER 8 COMMENTARY REFLECTIONS

1.   Which character traits make you a "great catch" for employers?

2.   Take a moment to review your resume. Does it include a solid listing of career accomplishments with measurable outcomes?

3.   Can you describe the "taste" or "flavor" that you want employers to have after reading your resume?

4. Ask your family, friends, and coworkers their thoughts about you and your work ethic. Record their comments here:

9

SIX TYPES OF RESUMES

"We all want progress, but if you're on the wrong road, progress means doing an about-turn and walking back to the right road; in that case, the man who turns back soonest is the most progressive." ~ C.S. Lewis

Knowing the best type of resume to use can determine the success of your job hunting efforts. Many resume writers and career coaches refer to only three major types. However, given the complexity of today's job market and, most importantly, the intricacies of each job seeker, it is prudent to flush out each kind of resume to determine which is best for your needs.

FUNCTIONAL

This format is often used to hide gaps in a resume and for people in career transition. Unfortunately, 99.95% of recruiters, hiring officials, and talent managers do not like functional resumes for that very reason. In addition, the functional resume highlights general work history traits in large summary- based paragraphs. Condensed text in a resume does not lend itself to easy reading or scanning and unfortunately sends up a "timeline" red flag. Remember, you only have ten seconds to make an impression. With that said, why would you expect the reader to try to connect the dots between when and where you performed what is listed on the resume? It is annoying and a waste of time. If you have nothing to hide, do you think that the functional resume is the best format to feature your brand? No. It is important to rediscover what makes you a good employee.

What are your strengths, passions, and talents? Once you have gone through the discovery process, you will be better equipped to put your personality on the page and go into future contact interviews with a positive sense of what to showcase versus the conventional approach of hiding past experiences that have contributed to a checkered employment history. Be positive. Don't hide-- highlight!

It is difficult for job seekers to penetrate today's market. My heart goes out to the countless professionals who find themselves looking for work after devoting decades to an employer. It is also difficult for recent college graduates who are competing with seasoned employees to get a foot in the door.

With that said, many people are bombarded with conflicting information on how best to market their skills on a resume. I know I should not get so worked up about which format a person chooses to brand her or his talent, but it really pulls at me when "career people" advise job seekers to use the Functional resume as the default resume type. Outdated and erroneous information is what forced me to create the Resume Branding approach to use the strengths of six resume formats to best market job seekers.

Now I'm aware of my quirky 29-year love affair with resumes and that it's an anomaly to say the least. However, I cringe every time I hear someone suggest the use of Functional formats. I stopped using them over fifteen years ago.

It is a huge disservice to paint the functional benefits of this old format with a broad brush. Just because it's an easier format for non-resume writers to remember does not mean it is the best way to highlight one's skills. With hundreds of applicants competing for the same position, it can be disastrous to try to lump all of your employment history together.

Here is why Functional resumes earn the F-Grade:

1. This format is often used to hide gaps in a resume by individuals who are in career transitions from dealing with challenging circumstances such as, incarceration, drug rehabilitation and poor job choices. Unfortunately, 99.95% of recruiters, hiring officials, and talent managers know that career personnel use this tactic to camouflage problematic information and do not like summary based formats for that reason They can read between the lines!

2. The Functional resume highlights general work history traits in large paragraphs. Condensed text in a resume does not lend itself to easy reading or scanning, and unfortunately sends up a "timeline" red flag. Remember, you only have seconds to make an impression.

3. It forces the reader to try to connect the dots between

when and where you performed what is listed on your resume. The goal is to create an "employer-friendly" resume that invites them to hire you.

If you have nothing to hide, do you think that the Functional resume is the best format to feature your brand?

CHRONOLOGICAL

In my experience, I find that the chronological resume is a method used to create a "mini-job description;" therefore, it fails to add personality. It's not as bad as the Functional resume but it most resembles a job application with a heavy emphasis on filling in the blanks. For example, if you use former job descriptions as the basis of your resume, then whoever assumed similar roles will have the same resume. Basically, if you take your name off the documents, 90% of the people you are competing with can put their names on your document. That's not a good look!

Chronological resumes earn a D grade. Here is why:

1. This format mirrors content on a job application. It traditionally goes back ten years and records the most recent position first. Unlike the functional resume, the chronological format lists when and where responsibilities and duties were performed in reverse chronological order. This makes it much easier to discern a job seeker's work history, but it overlooks other critical aspects of Resume Branding.

2. The Chronological format lacks personality and key

accomplishments that set you apart from the competition. Most people use this format to copy and paste from random job descriptions to establish an applicant's qualifications versus competitive candidacy.

COMBINATION

This format is a mix between the functional and chronological resumes. The usage of summaries to highlight skills and detail each employment listing combines the benefits of both formats. Recruiters and hiring managers prefer combination resumes from people who have solid work histories. On the other hand, this type of resume lacks the structure to showcase a brand persona.

At Persona Affairs, we stopped using the combination resume format eleven years ago. We found it to be incomplete because it kept the "mini-job description" element of the previous two resume styles and did not address how to be competitive. Put Your Personality on Paper!

The Combination resumes earn a D- grade. Here is why:

1. It blends the weakest elements of the Functional ad Chronological resumes in attempts to complete the job application process. Overall it lacks personality and marketable elements that make you stand out above the competition.

The next two resume types are not necessarily poor formats to use. They are simply more detailed and require a different level of attention.

FEDERAL

This format is best used for applying to a federal position. It can be distributed both on paper and electronically via the USAJOBS Builder website. Federal resumes are more detailed and can be as long as five to seven pages. Writing this type of resume involves elements of a job application like your social security number, supervisor's name, and telephone number. It asks, "How many people did you supervise, if any? What was your salary for each position listed?" Also, your employment history is not limited to ten years.

In many cases, a written portion is required and every online application must be supported by situational examples detailing when, how, and where activities were performed, especially when "Knowledge, Skills, and Abilities" (KSAs) are required.

CURRICULUM VITAE

This format, commonly referred to as a "CV," has two distinct purposes: 1) it is an internationally recognized resume type, and 2) it is a resume used within academia. As a former international credentials evaluator for one of the top five MBA programs in the nation, I had the privilege of translating CVs to solicit professional employment histories for graduate school applicants, representing over 75 countries. In most cases, these documents shared the same length as the Federal resume.

Faculty is the largest group that uses curriculum

vitae in the US. They must use their CV's to successfully demonstrate their educational acumen, research interests, teaching philosophies, and publications.

RESUME BRANDING MATRIX™

This blended format has been designed to infuse the effective elements of classic resume writing techniques with innovative personal branding strategies in order to showcase a job hunter's career personality and market value. We have incorporated seventeen years of experience behind the hiring table, knowledge of operations, and conflict management expertise to streamline how top talent is discovered.

The Resume Branding Matrix™ brings out each individual's brand persona. It can be scanned in ten seconds or less, while infusing qualitative and quantitative experience to support actionable accomplishments. Now you are ready to move beyond merely qualifying for a job and begin competing for a higher salary!

CHAPTER 9 COMMENTARY REFLECTIONS

1. What type of resume do you have?

2. Are there design elements (such as bullets, bolding, lines) to guide readers' eyes through the document and highlight important content?

3. Are accomplishments separated from responsibilities?

PART II

STRATEGY

10

BRAND MARKET RESEARCH

"Research is formalized curiosity. It is poking and prying with a purpose."
~ Zora Neale Hurston

Defining what the job market is looking for is essential. Regardless of the industry, if you have been in the same profession for several years, you know that the market is forever changing. Companies always make adjustments in personnel, technology, or protocols. A static market is a dead market. So if you want to stay relevant, you must go back to the drawing board and figure out how to sharpen your tools. In the case of Career Branding, it is time to start looking at the job boards and company websites.

What are administrative assistants doing these days? Are they working on Microsoft operating systems such as Windows Vista or the newly released Windows 8? Well, take a moment to find the comparison between the two, or vie for the opportunity to start working on them by taking continuing education courses from your local community college or career center. In the old days, some people would join a temporary or employment agency to get the chance to master the next level of software. Remember, companies base employment and salary on your brand value. Always look for opportunities to invest in yourself by participating in online or on-campus classes.

Brand market research is the method used to identify themes of needs and qualifications for each industry. The first phase in gathering career information is the decoding phase. Start by searching job descriptions for each position of interest to reveal a common thread of responsibilities. Even if it feels like this common thread is a needle in a haystack, it can still be found with the keenest eye. It is important for one to fully understand the needs of the market before starting the Resume Branding process. Another difference between traditional resume writing and the Resume Branding Matrix™ is that the latter is employer-friendly and puts the market into the product.

The worst thing for an employer or hiring manager to discover while reading a resume is that a person misinterpreted the job description or, in many cases, cut and pasted a few terms from the job posting into the resume. Do not do it.

Take the time to apply for positions that appear to be a good fit. Research the industry and, most importantly, the company of interest. What is the corporate culture like? Have you read the company blog or checked out its website? What is the constant trend? Is it customer care and staff development, or are they hiring from within? Being aware of your business environment preference is key to exploring which companies are potentially good fits for future opportunities; it is best to have a sense of where you are setting your sights. In conducting market research, you can gain an accurate idea of what employers consider to be top talent.

Unfortunately, a job description is just that--a description. It is challenging to discover which sets of key phrases are required for each industry. It may not be feasible to locate all the necessary clues in just one job description. Identifying key functions and levels of expertise for each trade is imperative.

APPROACH TO DISCERNING POSTS

A job description is a generic form of outlining the expectations needed to be a successful new employee. However, these expectations are often contrived and cut and pasted from other descriptions, without giving a clear and practical idea of what it is like to work for a particular company.

How does one employer match with your idea of a healthy workplace? Well, first you must decide which environments are best for you to thrive in. Do you prefer open and inviting work settings which allow you to bring your own solutions to problems and showcase your professional judgment? Or do you need a micromanaged or heavily controlled environment such as General Motors or McDonald's company, where the product goals are consistent due to scientifically researched outcomes that employ Six Sigma methodologies?

For example, in 2009, Amazon bought online shoe retailer Zappos for 880 million dollars. One of the determining factors included Zappos' CEO, Tony Hsieh. He was an innovative leader who infused exceptional customer care into each transaction and cultivated an employment environment that appreciated workers' unique personalities. This meant that they were encouraged to decorate their work spaces. Hsieh even occupied a cubicle as well. The company offered all new employees up to $1,000 to leave if they were not committed to putting customers first. This approach to corporate culture proved successful by Amazon's agreement to keep all employees after the merger. Amazon knew the depths to which Zappos went when they screened each person for their dedication to customer service.

When researching job descriptions, the underlining goal is to locate the common thread of responsibility. The purpose is to identify essential functions based on position, level, and corporate culture. Several job boards such as Indeed.com, CareerBuilder.com, and Linkup.com are excellent sources to explore.

Take a moment and think about how many positions you've applied for. Why do you think your success rate is not as high as expected?

Maybe you've reached a snag in your job search strategy. Well, let's jump right into why your new job is still waiting to meet you:

Pitfall #1: Using a Few Key Words to Qualify

It is easy to scan through hundreds of job descriptions, locate a few key words, and then voila, find that a new job opportunity appears. Job descriptions are treated like a recipe for employment. But the big question is, how often do people invest time in understanding what employers are looking for and matching their personal brand to each position?

Personal Branding reflects the essence of an individual; your personality, credentials, experience, and attire--. It applies principles that are similarly used for marketing commercial products and services; in this case, self-marketing. Basically, it is how you market yourself to employers and how you prove that you're the best candidate for the position.

Pitfall #2: Failing to Conduct Market Research

Many times people use job descriptions too literally and do not take the time to research companies to see if they're a fit. Most people are in such of a hurry to get a job, any job, that they overlook the importance of positioning themselves to compete instead of simply qualifying for a role.

As a job seeker, you want the intricacies of your career personality to resonate with the employer. Take the time to study the corporate portrait through 10-K reports, annual snapshots of the company's financial performance, and website career pages. How does your past or current experience fit into the job description? Will your talents and accomplishments shine on an application and distinguish you from competitors? If the answer is not a definitive "Yes," then you're increasing the chances of being turned down-- time and time again.

It's not enough to simply qualify for a job. You have to prove that you're the best at what you do. Invest in defining your personal brand so you can move from merely a qualified candidate to the top candidate for the position.

How do you define your personal brand and become the top candidate?

Pitfall #3: The Generic Resume

One hurdle to overcome is the process of submitting a resume and, ultimately, creating a unique first impression. A resume is your first interview and opportunity to present your personal brand to an employer. Within the first ten seconds, the resume should indicate why you are applying for the position and how you're the best candidate.

After reading tens of thousands of resumes, there appears to be a unique pattern between professionals with PHD's and those with No D's. The job descriptions and templates of the latter tend to dictate the course of the resume, rather than the candidate's brand persona, competence, ability to promote oneself, and career goals.

If everyone is using the same Microsoft template, then how can anyone stand out? Basically, most job seekers are just trying to qualify for each position they apply to. That is not enough.

One of the main reasons why people struggle with the concept of updating their resumes is the fact that they have undetermined directions and self-purposes. In order to effectively brand your resume, you must first conduct market research on the company you want to work forand perform an internal audit of your career goals. You should then be able to explain, with precision and clarity, what type of job you are seeking, what value you'd bring to the company, and most importantly, why the employer should choose you.

Resume Branding Is the Solution

When I created the Resume Branding Philosophy™ in 2007, it was designed to help all levels of professionals brand their work experiences and produce " employer-friendly" documents. With Resume Branding, the ultimate goal is to invite everyone who touches the document to hire you after reading your brand story.

In order to win your next job, you have to compete for it. How? By having an accomplishment-driven resume that showcases your personal brand. What have you done that's gone above and beyond what you were hired to do? How much money did you save past employers? Can you demonstrate your leadership ability? Resume Branding works because we ask detailed questions for you to rediscover your work contributions and expertise. We understand that most people go to work, do a great job, hope for that promotion, and start all over again. Resume Branding puts your ability to promote yourself in front.

Resume branding is just the start of establishing your skill sets and exceptional qualities. Once you have a brand story, you need to take it a step further by promoting it on social media through sites like LinkedIn, Facebook, and Twitter. This will allow recruiters to find you and examine whether or not you are a good fit for their companies. Additionally, when you use social media to engage followers and friends, your audience will perceive you as a subject matter expert (SME) who can build trust and share invaluable expertise.

The community needs to see why you are a preferable resource, and social media is the perfect outlet for generating mass exposure in a short amount of time. Develop your brand story based on past accomplishments, define your long and short term goals, and establish an online presence that will vastly increase your chances of being spotted by recruiters who are seeking out your talents.

Begin the resume branding process, and let this be the end of your job search.

CHAPTER 10 COMMENTARY REFLECTIONS

1. Can you locate which terms are required to be considered a qualified applicant for the job you seek?

2. Identify specific career experiences that will make you a stand out as a top candidate.

3. Visit a few job boards and company websites and list your findings here:

11

RESUME BRANDING MATRIX™

The Format

"Don't be a blueprint. Be an original." ~Roy Acuff

Our Resume Branding Matrix™ formats are built on honesty and trust. We focus on highlighting your brand essence, skill sets, and talents, versus hiding life challenges and responsibilities within the top fourth of the page. The Resume Branding Matrix™ shifts the focus from writer to reader. Administrators often have the added responsibility of reviewing resumes to fill vacant or newly created positions. It is rare to find "Professional Resume Readers" whose sole responsibility is to sort through hundreds of resumes. Therefore, composing a document with the hiring manager in mind is essential to getting it noticed immediately.

The ultimate goal is to create a resume that lets your

brand persona jump off the page. A sprinkling of keywords will not do the trick. It is easy to make a resume look nice, but it is harder to utilize the proper dosage of demonstrable accomplishments to support a professional brand. A customized letterhead on cream or lightly colored bond paper should be used on branded resumes, cover letters, and other corresponding documents. Copy paper is good for copiers, but not for presenting professionally customized resumes.

The Resume Branding Matrix™ format allows for a nice polish to any submission, whereas Microsoft Word templates do not. Take a moment to think about the billions of people who have access to Microsoft documents. If you use this program, you are not fully taking advantage of the personal branding process.

Templates force professionals to reduce their expertise to minuscule terms to comply with the template's functional and chronological structure. Seasoned employees need two pages to properly disperse their expertise. The old myth that resumes must be one page is catastrophic for professionals with a history of solid work. In many cases, people are forced to condense long paragraphs of information into tiny fonts to pack everything in. Fundamentally speaking, the single page requirement was a way to minimize lengthy storylines within the initial screening phase. I agree that applicants should use concise methods to tell their brand stories; however, you defeat the purpose of including your accomplishments and work history if they do not appeal to the reader.

Each section in the Resume Branding Matrix™ format is designed to take the benefits from each of the five other resume types and compose a resume with the end reader and the decision maker in mind. It uses opportunities to add your personality and market value into a well-branded document.

This portion of the guidebook explains the "how" and, most importantly, the "why not" in developing a strong resume brand.

CONTACT INFORMATION

When we look at Resume Branding, we can easily make a connection between ourselves and how we prefer to be reached. However, it is easy to abuse this section with irrelevant and unprofessional information. Let's take a look at each Resume Branding Matrix™ component:

NAME RECOGNITION

People often use a template to complete the resume requirements and fail to make their name a decent font size. Names should be the largest part of the resume since the person is the most important component of the process. Our suggestion is that it be between the font sizes of eighteen to twenty-two. Caution: do not make the size monstrous just for the sake of complying with our size suggestions; remain conservative and base it on the font type used. For example, **Verdana** is a san serif font, which is round and wide and is best used in size 10 font whereas **Garamond** is an elegant, narrow, old style serif font that can be used in a 11 or 12 size font. The sans serif fonts are preferred by recruiters because they are smartphone and iPad-friendly. In addition, if you are not in a creative industry, leave graphics and colors to a minimum. Graphics cannot overcome substance.

ADDRESS ME PROPERLY

The recent need for professionals to move to more prosperous parts of the country has created a major controversy about whether or not to put a home address on a resume. Some resume writers and career coaches have advised job seekers to either list post office boxes in lieu of a home address or leave off the address entirely to avoid discrimination. Although it sounds harsh, the rationale behind omitting an address to fool an employer in hopes of getting a job is unwise. The companies that may be holding special consideration for local applicants have the right to impact their local economy. Some may be receiving government contracts for hiring in economically-disadvantaged neighborhoods and need applicant addresses to maintain eligibility.

It would be better to indicate that you are willing to incur relocation expenses versus being deceptive. Consequently, opting to leave off an address sends up a huge "dishonesty" red flag. Remember, you only have ten seconds to make an impression. Why would you want the reader to start the screening process with question marks? A hiring manager will think, "If you cannot trust me with your address, then why should I trust what is on your resume?"

PHONE HOME?

Something as simple as a telephone number is often overlooked in the contact section. Use the best contact number and indicate whether the number is a mobile or residential number.

Why should this be important? As a hiring manager, there were occasions when I had to sort through hundreds of resumes and needed to hire someone, immediately. I In some instances, it was easier to contact a potential candidate at 7:30 p.m. on her or his mobile phone rather than calling the candidate at home and disrupting family time. If I called a mobile number, I also felt confident that the applicant would respond promptly rather than waiting until the following day.. It's all in the details. Take a little time to make it easier for the next step to begin.

E-MAIL BRAND

Beyond your name and phone number, an e-mail address is an easy way to add personality to your document. However, it could create the wrong reaction if misused. Keep your e-mail consistent with your name. Oprah Winfrey recently did a show on people who have same names and the ironic similarities between each other. One of the guests met seven other men who shared his name. We are well aware of how tedious it might be to create an e-mail address uniquely for you. But you must also take into consideration how challenging it is to make a memorable impression. The important term is "memorable." You also want to be remembered in a favorable light; therefore, including an e-mail address with sexual, humorous, and inappropriate names is not advised. Rather than being known by your favorite body part or animal preference via an e-mail address, save it for the water cooler once you are hired.

Overall, the contact section should not exceed three lines in order to maximize space and balance the amount of white space between it and your job-related information. In addition, make sure you create a header for the second page in the event that it gets displaced. I remember when my administrative assistant misplaced the first page of a potential candidate's resume. Fortunately, the job seeker listed contact information on the second page. We were able to schedule an on-campus interview and the candidate was savvy enough to bring more resume copies on the day of the interview. Thankfully, we could save face and the person got the job!

NAME
Address
E-mail/Phone (Type)

Name   Page 2
E-mail/Phone # (Preferably Mobile)

OBJECTIVE STATEMENTS

"To have or not to have?" This question regarding an objective statement is still a troubling debate for many job seekers. I stopped using them over fifteen years ago, because, in most cases, they are generic statements used to declare what the job applicant wants. The typical statement reads: "How I want to use my current position as a stepping stone to meet my personal goals." Unfortunately, the candidate has yet to say why a hiring manager should hire him or her. Employers want to know what you are going to offer them.

Objective statements take up the most valuable space on the document. I often tell clients that they have not been invited to the negotiation table to say what they want. Tell employers who you are and why you think you are a good fit for their companies so that they can invite you to the bargaining table. I often use the example of an employer potentially not giving you a promotion, but maybe offering you a $15,000 raise. Which one would you prefer? It is obvious that your objective is to get the job. Remember, you only have ten seconds to get noticed, and the initial goal is to introduce your brand as the top candidate.

Substitute what you want with what you can offer and then the reader will have a better idea of whether or not you can pass the first interview. If you are still an objective statement fan, then switch the focus to what you can offer potential employers. Convert it into a personal brand statement, highlighting your transferable skill sets.

SUM OF ALL PARTS

Our more functional alternative to the age-old objective statement is a "Summary of Qualifications," which is better suited to introduce a personal brand. We suggest listing four to five statements highlighting your most attractive transferable skill sets. It is best to start by converting statements into a thirty second commercial format about past experiences, level of expertise, and personal strengths. Keep in mind you only have seconds to get your resume in the interview stack. The brand story should be scaled down into a summary, which will translate well into a cover letter and set the overall tone of the resume.

Provide a sales pitch narrowing your professional focus and goals for future employment. In business, this is what we call an elevator pitch. Using a summary or profile format will assist in a quick scan. In addition, you can include experiences from a job not listed on your resume, due to the "ten years or newer" preference.

ELEVATOR PITCH

If the opportunity for you to meet the hiring manager of your choice presented itself, what would you say? How would you say it? That is what we want you to consider when fine tuning your elevator pitch for future employment. Do not take yourself for granted. In other words, how do you put your best foot forward?

Employers need to know what you are bringing to the table and what makes you special. This elevator pitch is a practical way for you to cleanly and concisely make your case for why and how you can meet the next employment opportunity. Create a pitch that invites a person to offer you a business card or ask for yours.

SUMMARY OF QUALIFICATIONS EXAMPLE

Successful leadership experience in financial aid, admissions, recruitment, and enrollment services within a university setting. Demonstrated expertise in organizational development and brand operations. Exceptional problem solver with precise communication that translates into memorable experiences with students, parents, and academic professionals.

CORE ELEMENTS

The "Core Competencies" section, also known as "Areas of

Expertise," is designed to list the key tenets of your work experience without littering the resume with buzzwords just for effect. The maximum words or terms can range from six to nine disciplines in three columns, to provide a quick list of skill sets. If the core competencies section is centered, the reader will gravitate toward it.

CORE COMPETENCIES

Sales	Operations	Recruitment
Marketing	Customer Care	Quality Control

Listing areas of expertise will satisfy both visual and electronic scanning systems. This format will give recruiters and human resource managers a quick snapshot of your credentials and encourage them to pull you out of the crowd of resumes into the interview stack.

EDUCATION ESSENTIALS

Far too often, people opt to put their education at the bottom or, worse yet, on the second page. As a benchmark, if you have the minimum education requirements for a job, list it under the "Core Competencies" area. It presents the reader with the fact that you qualify for the vacant position in a quick glance. In addition, it affords her or him a chance to see if you have graduated from a prestigious institution and if you are in the industry.

For job seekers who graduated years ago, it has often been advised to omit dates to avoid discrimination. I cannot stress enough that if information is omitted, you run the risk of offending your potential employer because you do not trust the employer to be fair. In addition, do you really want to work for a company that is more interested in your age than what you have to offer?

As a businessperson, the market is great for employers who need experienced talent ready to hit the ground running and perform beyond what they were hired to do. On the other hand, some people are ashamed of their lack of education. There is a quote by the Greek poet Agathon: "Even God cannot change the past." With that said, the Resume Branding Strategy™ allows you to place the "Education" section in the area you are most comfortable with. However, I also hold strongly to the idea that whatever level of education you have acquired, it has attributed to your success.

Do not mimic an ostrich and put your head in the sand. Get accepted to a college or trade school and add this information to your resume; continue to invest in your brand value.

EDUCATION EXAMPLE

FORDHAM UNIVERSITY   New York, NY
Master of Science in Communications   June 1999

COMPUTER BASICS

At Persona Affairs we prefer not to use the term "Technical Skills" or "Computer Skills." Computer knowledge is a stronger interpretation of diverse levels of software ability. This is the first section of the resume in which I would add bullet points. Templates and resume writers tend to "over-bullet" resumes. Everything has a bullet indicator; therefore, nothing stands out. In the Resume Branding Matrix,™ bullets are reserved to bring direct attention to areas that can be easily read within ten seconds while multi-tasking, such as reviewing documents while talking on the phone. Remember, most companies do not have a designated "Resume Reader" to handle the screening process.

COMPUTER KNOWLEDGE EXAMPLE

- Adobe Acrobat
- Microsoft Access
- Lotus Notes
- Microsoft Excel
- Microsoft Word
- Peoplesoft

PROFESSIONAL CREDENTIALS

Based on your expertise, your resume can be up to two pages long. We have a saying at Persona Affairs: " Everyone scans the first page; give them a reason to look at the second." You highlight your diverse skill sets if you outline each job position separately. For greater impact, list each position and include departmental information within three to four statements, highlighting the most relative elements from your job description. When you apply to a position, you are expected to have a certain skill set. A few of the items listed below can be transferred into this area. One goal is to provide a snapshot of the company culture while adding personality to the document. If you supervised staff members, indicate the positions they held.

Another objective is to make your resume brand quantitative and qualitative. It brings personality into the document and a snapshot of your past and current work environments.

Simplified example:

Receptionist #1:

Answered phones, greeted guests, and typed letters

VS.

Receptionist #2:

Managed a 24- line switchboard and provided reception for 500 international diplomats and C-level guests. Generated reports using Microsoft Excel spreadsheets for the Vice President of Operations.

Please consider a cleaner format to highlight your position and the brand value of your corporate expertise:

BANK OF AMERICA   Charlotte, NC
Financial Analyst   2006 – Present

ACCOMPLISHMENT-DRIVEN LIFE

As mentioned earlier in this section, you want to have a refreshed take on what you have done beyond your hired duties. An "accomplishments" area on your resume also provides an opportunity for you to bring your personality into the document, an action which ultimately makes you more competitive. Think about the internal and external tools you use to get your job done. How do you handle crises and conflicts? How do you demonstrate professional judgment in your industry? How do you handle a weak team member and ensure a positive outcome for a team project? Provide employers with a visual image of your accomplishments. Draw the reader into the window of your previous and current employers' operations without divulging company secrets. Answer some of the standard behavioral interview questions with your resume.

The "Accomplishments" section is the second area within the Resume Branding Matrix™ that should be in bullets. You want the reader's attention to be drawn to your accomplishments. Unlike many resumes which start off with centered accomplishments, it is much easier to document success if this area is a subset of the "Professional Experience" section. This format draws from the benefits of a combination resume, using descriptive terminology to express why you are a good fit for the job available.

Examine the purpose behind including certain information on a resume. Who benefits: the hiring manager or yourself? In this area, list the things you've created or performed that were above and beyond what you were hired to do and include the impact of your accomplishments; if you can't state an impact, then the reader will ask why it is important. Have the reader in mind and not your self-esteem!

Simplified example:

Streamlined filing area from numeric to alpha system

VS.

Planned and organized more orderly filing system for over 450,000 records. Implementation of manual tracking process reduced misfiled documents by 30%.

PROFESSIONAL PERSONALITY

If many years have elapsed since your last academic venture and you have not obtained a degree, you may complement your education with a "Professional Development" section. When Delta Airlines merged with Northwest Airlines, employees from both companies were given the chance to re-evaluate their market value for the largest airline in the world. I had the pleasure of consulting a group of Delta professionals who were in the unique situation of needing to rebrand themselves for a company for which they had, in some cases, worked for over twenty years. In addition, not only were they competing with their local colleagues for positions they currently held, but also with Delta employees worldwide and external job seekers who were interested in joining the company's elite brand of personnel.

Many of Delta's personnel were hired soon after high school or college and never composed a resume or needed additional documentation beyond the standard application. In the past, they had a very impromptu interviewing process that was not as competitive as ones in today's job market. Therefore, the task of jumping into a bilateral employment process was extremely difficult for them. With Resume Branding, they were able to market their uniquely diverse personalities and brand loyalty toward Delta, while reintroducing their brand value to people they work with every day. Once Delta's staff embraced the Resume Branding Matrix™ they were not only able to add personality by outlining their individual accomplishments, but also they began to view their contributions and internal training in a different light.

Adding the "Professional Development" section demonstrates to employers that you have consistently reinvested in your education and trade value. We use this section to assist employees who have not completed a degree program.

During the 2008 presidential election David Plouffe, the former campaign director for then- Senator Barack Obama, admitted that he was pursuing his first bachelor's degree at the University of Delaware (UD) after twenty years. President-elect Obama credited Plouffe in his acceptance speech, calling him "the unsung hero of this campaign, who built the ". . .best political campaign, I think, in the history of the United States of America." In addition, Plouffe's Republican counterpart Steve Schmidt, who helped run Senator John McCain's presidential campaign, also recently earned his bachelor's degree from the University of Denver. They both graduated in 2010.   Obviously education is important, but it does not trump all abilities. Take credit for what professional development and on-the-job training you have acquired and include it on your resume.

Here is a short list of notable people who did not earn a college degree and changed the world despite of it:

Richard Brandson – Founder of Virgin Airlines
Bill Gates – Founder of Microsoft
Steve Jobs – Founder of Apple
Mark Zuckerberg – Founder of Facebook
Rachael Ray – Cooking Personality without formal culinary training
Maya Angelou – Writer who never attended college, but earned numerous honorary doctoral degrees

As a former Assistant Director of Admissions, I had the opportunity to see a variety of academic transcripts, each telling its own story. Part of my responsibility was to interpret candidates' educational abilities and determine if they could successfully pursue one of our bachelor or graduate degree programs. With that said, it was the job of the applicant to explain low grades, lengthy gaps, and why he or she matriculated to four or more universities without acquiring a degree. After years of working in admissions, I realized that life happens to everyone and, in many cases, our educations take a back seat. Remember my brand story and how I followed my mother's footsteps and graduated college as a non-traditional student? I have built this perspective into the Resume Branding Matrix™ specifically to address the guilt and shame of people without four-year degrees.

PROFESSIONAL DEVELOPMENT EXAMPLE

INSTITUTION/COMPANY   City/State
Courses   Dates

ADDITIONAL INFORMATION

There are always opportunities to structure additional brand value and personality into the Resume Branding Matrix™. Some job seekers are members of organizations or affiliates with associations and sit-on boards. It is imperative to include this information in a clean and concise manner. The same is true if you are an overachiever and have been recognized for it.

Sample Formats:

AFFILIATIONS AND ASSOCIATIONS

The U.S. Chamber of Commerce, Small Business Board
American Business Women's Association, Vice President

AWARDS AND HONORS

Top Sales Agent, 2008

COMMUNITY OUTREACH

Include volunteer experiences that can directly speak to the position sought. List the company, agency or organization, role, and year(s) or participation. This is a great area to align your personal brand with an employer who has a strong interest in social responsibility.

Habitat for Humanity – Veterans Build, ReStore - 2013

REFERENCES FOR LATER

The "References" section is no longer required on a resume. If the company asks for your references as a supplement within the application process, comply with the request; if not, provide them at a later date.

When submitting your references, set up an additional page with the same header as that on your resume. Recently, some employers have been screening references before contacting the applicant. I am not in favor of this practice and strongly believe that the applicant should be considered to be a viable candidate first before contacting her or his references.

RESUME BRANDING MATRIX FORMAT™

NAME
Address
Phone (Type) ∞ Brand Email

SUMMARY OF QUALIFICATIONS

~~~~~~

~~~~~~

~~~~~~~~~~~~~~~~~~~~~~~

CORE COMPETENCIES

----------------- ------------------- ------------------

----------------- ------------------- ------------------

EDUCATION
INSTITUTION   City/State
Degree/Degree Program   Month/Year

COMPUTER KNOWLEDGE
◊ Software   ◊ Software   ◊ Software
◊ Software   ◊ Software   ◊ Software

PROFESSIONAL EXPERIENCE
COMPANY/ORGANIZATION   City/State
Position or Title   Month/Year
~~~~~~

~~~~~~

~~~~~~~~~~~~~~~~~~~~~~~

   ◊ Accomplishment ~~ Impact
   ◊ Accomplishment ~~ Impact

PROFESSIONAL DEVELOPMENT ~ (Optional)

AFFILIATIONS & ASSOCIATIONS ~ (If applicable)
CERTIFICATIONS ~ (If applicable)
AWARDS & HONORS ~ (If applicable)
COMMUNITY OUTREACH ~ (If applicable)

CHAPTER 11 COMMENTARY REFLECTIONS

1. When you look at your contact information, is it complete?

2.   What steps do you need to take to make your contact information support your branding process?

3. What statements would best describe your skills, talents, and professional aspirations?

4.   In your past experience, what would stand out to a potential employer?

5.   What company(s) do you wish to work for? Why does their corporate culture appeal to you?

6.   Can you narrow down your brand story to twenty words or less?

7.   Do you have experience from more than one industry that can make you competitive?

8.   What area of expertise do you most connect with?

9.   Are you in transition? If yes, which skills are most needed in the next role you want to assume?

10. List six to nine core competency areas.

11. What internal and external classes or courses have you taken to strengthen your brand?

12. Which classes would you like to take to add value to a potential employer?

13.   Can you list two to three accomplishments for each of your previous positions? If yes, include projects or tasks that went above and beyond what you were hired to do. If no, then answer the questions listed in the Accomplished-Driven Life Section.

Position #1

Position #2

Position #3

Position #4

12

TECH YOUR BRAND ON THE ROAD

Social Networking

"Knowing is not enough; we must apply. Willing is not enough; we must do."
~ Johann Wolfgang von Goethe

In the 2008 presidential race, social media marketing strategies sparked grass roots efforts to galvanize people to act while setting a new standard for how future political campaigns should be run. Obama, who was the relatively unknown candidate, was affiliated with sixteen different social networking sites. Each site was representative of diverse segments of the United States' population and international community.

Unbeknownst to Obama's opponents and many in the public, the cofounder of Facebook opted to step down from his post and join Barack Obama's campaign, thus lending his expertise to designing the MyBO.org site, which allowed supporters to meet and greet each other, host political house parties, register voters, schedule door-to-door campaign activities, and most of all, generate the largest amount of incremental political contributions to date.

According to the Federal Elections Commission, President Barack Obama raised over 744 million dollars in 2008 and later surpassed 1 Billion in 2012. With these facts in mind, I decided to join thirteen of those social networks to establish a stronger brand presence online and position myself to assist people in career transition around the globe. After all, if then-Senator Barack Obama could become President of the United States and the leader of the free world by social networking, then surely people can find jobs using the same methodology. After all, the political campaign is similar to a lengthy application and interview process for a job. Obama was essentially a job seeker, like many people today, and by using a few tools from his strategy, you can reach the same outcome.

Microsoft also recognized the power of social networks by buying 1.6% of Facebook's stock for 240 million dollars in October 2007. What does this tell job seekers? You should use your time and energy to get your brand on the social network highway.

Google your name and check the results. Are you listed at the top of the search? If yes, is it a favorable result? If not, it's time to invest in developing an engaging career brand and positioning yourself to compete for the next job opportunity. Update your resume and create an online profile to invite employers to hire you today!

Become familiar with some of the major networking sites, such as Facebook, Twitter, Google+ and LinkedIn. My favorite site for people who are unemployed, underemployed, and in career transition is LinkedIn. This site is strictly for professional purposes. LinkedIn has thousands of groups to join that will keep you abreast of industry information and job offerings. It is also a great resource to ask questions and generate discussions with experts and leaders in any given field. When you engage frequently with other members within a group, the system will acknowledge you as a subject matter expert (SME) and herald you as the "Top Influencer" in the group.

Blogs are also useful tools to engage readers in your trade, expand your digital voice, and establish higher levels of professional credibility. A blog gives you a cost-effective method to make connections with potential employers that can expand your brand, image, and readership. Decide whether you want to write blog articles daily, weekly or monthly. Once you choose the ideal frequency of publishing your opinions online, then consider submitting your work to industry publications to further amplify your personal brand.

In the age of identity theft, it is perfectly understandable for people to have reservations about what they put online. Unfortunately, most people never Google their names or addresses to see the information that is already out there. My father once gave a voice command to his Nook to find the directions to a relative's address, and guess what came up? Almost everything. The picture of the home, a 360° street view, a list of residents, and the value of the property. So be proactive and take control of your online presence.

Be sensible about your information. Consider attending networking events if social networking is not your preference. Nothing substitutes the power of making face-to-face connections. It is suggested that job seekers attend two networking events a week. Meetup.com is a nice starting place to find groups of interest. Look into non-job related groups as well. These groups will give you the opportunity to become comfortable talking about topics and activities you most enjoy, while providing an opportunity to share your job search goals.

Eventbrite.com is another great resource. Filter your search to free and minimal cost events in your area and start practicing your elevator pitch. Remember the goal is to build your network, not to guilt every person you meet into finding you a job.

CHAPTER 12 COMMENTARY REFLECTIONS

1.   List the social media sites you are signed up to. Which social networks do you feel most comfortable with?

2.   If you were to start a blog, what topic (s) would you write about?

3.   Go online and visit www.Meetup.com and browse through the various groups.   List a few groups that appeal to you.

4. Go online and visit www.linkedin.com and create a profile. Browse the various groups and list five groups that most appeal to you.

13

ENGAGEMENT

"The Pertinent Question is NOT how to do things right — but how to find the right things to do, and to concentrate resources and efforts on them."
~ Peter Drucker

As the years go on, I have found that I've transformed into a movie buff. Not the type that remembers every line of a film, but one who recalls a segment or two in a great film. I've also experienced many unsuspecting career-related "Aha!" moments.

It was a week night and I was flipping through the TV channels. I stumbled across a film gem called *Shawshank Redemption*, starring Tim Robbins (Andy Defresne) and Morgan Freeman (Ellis Boyd 'Red' Redding). The 1994 picture is set in a 1920's jail, and Andy, the lead character, is a former banker who has been framed for killing his wife. He is deemed guilty and earns two life-sentences without possibility of parole. During his sentence, Andy meets Red, who is an inmate serving a life sentence for murder. The unlikely pair became friends.

Anticipate a better outcome

What intrigued me most about this film is that Andy not only maintained his innocence, but he also maintained his persona throughout his years in prison. How did he do it? He held on to what jail could never take away from him-- hope.

Deep down inside, each of us has the inner strength to hope for a better future. Hope for the return of the pre-recession days when the value of a house was soaring and the job market was not crippled by the suffering economy.

Do not get stuck in the past

Which brings me to another character in the movie named "Brooks" (played by James Whitmore); he reminded me of the modern day job seeker. Brooks, the jail librarian, had been incarcerated for fifty years and was granted release after serving his time. Upon his release, he panicked and tried to kill a fellow inmate in an attempt to stay locked up. Imagine being immersed into the workplace after half a century in jail. The world is likely to be a scary place. Thankfully, Red was able to calm Brooks down and help him rejoin society.

Your first attempt should not be your last

With limited resources, Brooks managed to find a job as

a bag packer at a grocery store and a room at a halfway house, compliments of the judicial system. After his abrupt life change, Brooks was scared of all the new things that came along with a progressive society. Cars had changed, houses were different, and technology made everything smaller and faster. Sadly, Brooks committed suicide because the change was too unbearable.

Embrace a new employment strategy

Many job seekers are feeling the pain of progress and killing their chances of getting hired fast. They have not incorporated personal branding strategies into their job search toolkit. Social media plays a large role in landing a job. LinkedIn is the best professional social media platform for employers to connect with job seekers.

The best LinkedIn profiles comprise a synopsis of the personal brand. An updated resume is the best complement to a digital profile; they go hand-in-hand. It's easy to glance at a person's LinkedIn profile and see if he or she is interested in career opportunities, contributing to group discussions, and receiving recommendations. However, most members just sign up, upload their resumes, and wait for someone to request a connection. LinkedIn is a serious professional networking tool and therefore, requires time and effort in order to build an effective profile.

LinkedIn has added new features, including the LinkedIn Today online newspaper, which helps users engage with companies, conduct market research, and follow industry trends. 89% of recruiters are on LinkedIn, and countless others are using social media to source talent. Meet them where they are. Engage them with your expertise and personality. Brand yourself to stand out from the crowd.

If you're looking for a job, start using LinkedIn before, during, and after your job search. Real Names, Real Companies, Real Jobs...Really!

14

TIPS TO MAKE A JOB FAIR
WORK FOR YOU

"Do not wait to strike till the iron is hot; but make it hot by striking."
~ William B. Sprague

After speaking at numerous job fairs over the years about ways to brand your resume and improve you chances of getting hired, I found that job seekers have grown weary of mass job fairs. The numbers of attendees have dropped dramatically and unfortunately many have given up with the process altogether. Mostly because of the reality of being herded into long lines, just to be told to when you reach the front to apply online. It's frustrating to say the least, and probably has you asking why these companies are even wasting time, space, and money.

Well, they do it for a few reasons. Companies love to say that they are hiring because it is great PR and gets them instant visibility. A career fair is also a great way to get your brand message out to the public.

So the next time you hear a company is hosting a job fair, make sure you're prepared. Remember these seven keywords to help you navigate a career fair and get the most out of your time:

1. Research

Look at the career fair flyer or website to see which companies are attending. Are there five or fifty?

Decide what employers you want to work for. An "I'll take anything" approach will not do because you will be standing in every line and your job search will last longer than necessary.

2. Website

Go to the company websites and see what positions are available, if any.

Ask yourself, "Do they have positions that I am qualified for?" Focus on positions in which you will be able to compete for the top slot, and make a copy of the job descriptions for your records.

3. Apply

Once you've found a position you can compete for, apply online.

This does not defeat the purpose of going to the job

fair. Attendance adds a face to your application and piques the company representative's interest. Don't forget your elevator pitch!

4. Engage

Share your interest in the company and the position.

Tell the recruiter that you have applied online and ask if he or she has any other information to offer about the job. Ask questions like, "How soon are you hoping to fill the role? What is the best way to stay in contact with you? What is your ideal candidate?"

This is a great opportunity for you to get inside information.

5. Submit

Yes, give them another copy of your branded resume.

Please have it printed on bounded paper. Copy paper is for copiers. Present yourself as a professional by using quality resume paper. Cream is my favorite color because it will stand out among the hundreds of resumes the recruiter will receive that day.

I remember when my friend Diane asked me to update her resume. She went through our company's market-based questionnaire (normally forty to seventy questions long) and we used the Resume Branding Matrix format to finalize her document. After receiving the initial draft, she was ecstatic and said, "Wow, I want to hire myself!" That was the reaction we were looking for, but we advised her to review it for accuracy and to become familiar with her newly branded resume.

Let's just say that Diane could not get past her excitement and headed for a job fair right away. She stood in a long line to submit her resume to the recruiter. Once it was in the recruiter's hands, she turned to head to the next employer. To her surprise, the company representative started asking her questions about her managerial ability, noticing that she had experience in real estate, as well as in property management. Yes, they were listed in the Core Competencies section. The ten-second rule had worked.

Diane called me and said "Girl, I had to head to the nearest table and read your resume. I was so shocked that they asked me questions on the spot. I'm not going to be caught off guard again." The point of Diane's experience was that she had to revisit her brand story, not only for applying to jobs, but also for selling her talents and abilities. Resume Branding welcomes you to your market value.

6. Exchange

Attach your business or contact card to your resume (Yes, you should have a contact card to distribute even if you're not currently employed). There are a number of cost-effective companies that sell them for as low as $15 for 250 cards. Each card should include your name, email address, telephone number, and LinkedIn profile or website URL. If you spend a little extra, you can include a line or two from your summary of qualifications, i.e., your elevator pitch, on the back of the card. Do not forget to ask if you can have the company representative's card and if you can send a LinkedIn invitation to stay connected. Keep in mind that your online profile should complement your branded resume.

7. Follow Up

Send an email or social media message via Linked-In, Facebook, or Twitter. "Like" the company's posts, but only if you really do. Leave comments and follow the company on Linked-In to receive job updates and stay abreast of comings and goings.

Overall, preparation before attending a job fair is key. It provides a great reason to research a company's culture and make great connections with current employees. Take time beforehand to decide whether you should attend, then make the most of your time by using these tips.

The days of wasting your time going to a career fair and handing in your resume are over.

15

EPILOGUE

"Carpe Diem"—"Seize the day." ~ Unknown

How are you going to use what you have read in this book? It is time to make a choice to reclaim your value. You can't continue to let others dictate when and if you're promotable. If you're unemployed or underemployed, change your focus from your current status to your past performances, talents, and abilities. The economic meltdown gave all of us the opportunity to reevaluate our lives; how we spend our money, time, and most importantly, how we manage what we can control. With the help of social media, you can define your digital footprint and capture employers' attention by establishing an engaging personal brand that will change the course of your career.

NOTES

NOTES

NOTES

NOTES

NOTES

QUOTES

"Character is like a tree and reputation like a shadow. The shadow is what we think of it; the tree is the real thing."
~ Abraham Lincoln

"Philosophy is like trying to open a safe with a combination lock: each little adjustment of the dials seems to achieve nothing, only when everything is in place does the door open." ~ Ludwig Wittgenstein

"Our character is basically a composite of our habits. Because they are consistent, often unconscious patterns, they constantly, daily, express our character." ~ Stephen Covey

"Interview, Don't clamor for an interview. Instead search for the INNER VIEW. " ~ Sri Sathya Sai Baba

"Integrity is what we do, what we say and what we say we do." ~ Don Galer

"Looking back you realize that a very special person passed briefly through your life and it was you. It is not too late to find that person again." ~ Robert Brault

"If we all did the things we are capable of doing, we would literally astound ourselves." ~ Thomas A. Edison

"Try not to become a person of success, but try to become a person of value." ~ Albert Einstein

"We all want progress, but if you're on the wrong road, progress means doing an about-turn and walking back to the right road; in that case, the man who turns back soonest is the most progressive." ~ C.S. Lewis

"Research is formalized curiosity. It is poking and prying with a purpose." ~ Zora Neale Hurston

"Don't be a blueprint. Be an original." ~ Roy Acuff

"Knowing is not enough; we must apply. Willing is not enough; we must do." ~ Johann Wolfgang von Goethe

"The Pertinent Question is NOT how to do things right — but how to find the right things to do, and to concentrate resources and efforts on them." ~ Peter Drucker

"Do not wait to strike till the iron is hot; but make it hot by striking." ~ William B. Sprague

"Carpe Diem"—"Seize the day." ~ Unknown

ABOUT THE AUTHOR

"Your past does not define you---it refines you." ~KNC

Kim N. Carswell is the founder and Chief Executive Consultant at Persona Affairs, LLC, a personal branding firm that provides social media engagement services to job seekers, working professionals, and entrepreneurs.

Carswell is an engaging conversationalist and keynote speaker who uses her business acumen to counsel various commercial and educational institutions with career branding and social media needs. She is a well-respected personal brand architect and sits on numerous advisory boards, along with a number of the Top 50 corporations from Fortune 500's list.

In addition to Carswell's professional development background, she has coached executives and rising professionals game-changing insight and solutions about strengthening their digital presences. Carswell has also been selected to participate in beta testing for the top social media platforms worldwide and was awarded the "Top 1%" LinkedIn users' distinction in 2013.

For further information, or to book or talk with Mrs. Carswell, contact:

Persona Affairs, LLC
3900 Crown Road, #161870
Atlanta, GA 30321
engage@kimncarswell.com
888.331.4447
www.personaaffairs.com

CPSIA information can be obtained at www.ICGtesting.com
Printed in the USA
LVOW05s1322200414

382453LV00001B/21/P